Katie

Drawing Dinosaurs

Jerome Goyallon

Sterling Publishing Co., Inc. New York

To Pierre-Alexandre and Anne-Sophie
Philippe and Xavier
Nathalie and Francois
Anne-Marine, Sandy and Benjamin
Sylvain and Aurelie

Library of Congress Cataloging-in-Publication Data

Goyallon, Jerome.
    [Apprendre en dessinant les vértebrés primitifs. English]
    Drawing dinosaurs / Jerome Goyallon.
        p.   cm.
    Translation of: Apprendre en dessinant les vértebrés primitifs
and Apprendre en dessinant les dinosaures.
    Includes index.
    Summary: Presents facts about the anatomy and lifestyle of
dinosaurs and other extinct animals and provides instructions on how
to reproduce drawings of these creatures by hand or by computer.
    ISBN 0-8069-8742-1
    1. Dinosaurs in art—Juvenile literature.   2. Extinct animals in
art—Juvenile literature.   3. Drawing—Technique—Juvenile
literature. [1. Dinosaurs in art. 2. Extinct animals in art.
3. Drawing—Technique.] I. Title.
NC780.5.G6813 1993
    743′.6—dc20   93-2809
                                                     CIP
                                                     AC

English translation by Keith Schiffman

10 9 8 7 6 5 4 3 2 1

Published 1993 by Sterling Publishing Company, Inc.
387 Park Avenue South, New York, N.Y. 10016
Originally published in French by Éditions du B.R.G.M.
under the titles *Apprendre en Dessinant Les Vértebrés
Primitifs* © 1991 and *Apprendre en Dessinant Les Dinosaures*
© 1987 by Bureau de Recherches Géologiques et Minières
English translation © 1993 by Sterling Publishing Company, Inc.
Distributed in Canada by Sterling Publishing
% Canadian Manda Group, P.O. Box 920, Station U
Toronto, Ontario, Canada M8Z 5P9
Distributed in Great Britain and Europe by Cassell PLC
Villiers House, 41/47 Strand, London WC2N 5JE, England
Distributed in Australia by Capricorn Link Ltd
P.O. Box 665, Lane Cove, NSW 2066
Manufactured in the United States of America

Sterling ISBN 0-8069-8742-1

Contents

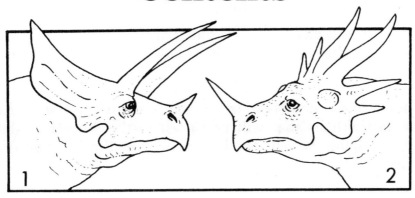

The Dinosaurs

and Their Ancestors

The Drawing

When you want to draw a picture that is based on another—like the dinosaurs and other creatures in this book—it helps to have lots of key points and guiding lines to follow.

One of the easiest ways to do it is to frame your creature in a square or rectangle. Then, you draw in the lines that will be closest to the dinosaur's shape. You can start by drawing in lines that cut the box in half (midlines) or go from corner to corner (diagonals)—

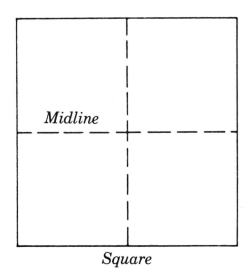

Square

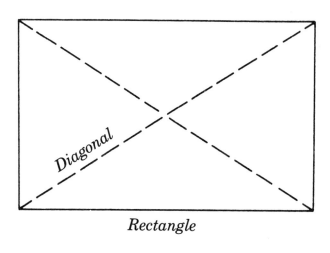

Rectangle

and then add lines that connect in other ways.

Using these guides, it's easy to do a new sketch that will end up as your final drawing. And you can make it any size you want.

For instance: If you use a frame in which the width of the box is twice the height, such as this one:

you can make it bigger just by doubling the width. You could make it

2 × 4 inches (5 cm × 10 cm) or
4 × 8 inches (10 cm × 20 cm) or
1 yard × 2 yards (1 m × 2 m) or

anything in between.

You could use a frame like this:

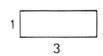

and make your drawing 2 × 6 inches (5 cm × 15 cm) and so on—as long as you keep the proportions the same.

How To Do It

1) Turn to any creature in this book. Then, using pencil, paper and a ruler, draw your frame—either a square or some other kind of rectangle—following the proportions shown on the page.

Draw in the midlines and diagonals that will guide you in making your sketch.

Now put the first lines in place, blocking in the major features of the animal—its body, tail, neck, and so on.

2) Following the original drawing shown in the book, add to the sketch, using the guidelines to help you get your lines in the right place. Don't hesitate to add other midlines and diagonals, if they'll help you block in your creature.

3) You can do your final drawing in ink or with a felt-tip marker after you erase any unneeded lines. Wait, though, till the ink is completely dry before you erase the frame and guidelines.

If you want to make the drawing even more your own, you can color it in—either in black and white or in color, as on the cover of this book. You can use pens for this, or watercolors, colored pencils or acrylics—or any other medium you want.

You can also draw the creatures in this book using a computer, a mouse, a software program or a fiber optic wand (a light pen). The instructions remain the same:

1) Outline the square or rectangle, as well as the midlines and diagonals, on the screen—in blue, for example.

2) Using another color—black, if you want—draw in the animal, line by line, following the original in the book.

3) When your drawing is complete, erase the blue lines (the frame and guidelines), and what remains will be your drawing, outlined in black, which you can keep.

You can go on coloring your drawing, or create a complete scene, or add figures to create a whole herd of creatures.

You can also draw several different animals side by side. If your software program will do animation, you can create a whole parade of extinct animals.

Dimetrodon,
drawn on a microcomputer
with a software program
by Pierre-Alexandre Goyallon.

Getting to Know the Dinosaurs

While you do your own drawing, you'll find out about each one of the dinosaurs.

Not all dinosaurs look alike, and you'll find creatures here that belong to different reptile families.

The word "dinosaur" is made up of two Greek words:
  deinos which means "terrible"
  saura which means "lizard"
That's why so many dinosaur names end with "saurus." It tells us that they belong to the lizard group.

You'll also find an English translation of the dinosaurs' Latin names, so that you can see what they mean.

For example, *Anatosaurus* means "duck lizard." When you see its head, you'll understand why it got this name.

The scientific name (*Anatosaurus*) is universal. It's the same name all over the world. Every species of animal and every vegetable on earth has a scientific name that is the same in every country.

Dinosaurs are classed in two groups. These groups are called "orders."

1) In the *Ornithischian* order, the animals' hindquarters are like those of birds. The *ornithischians* were all plant eaters.

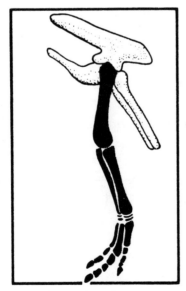

Ornithischians
bird-hipped

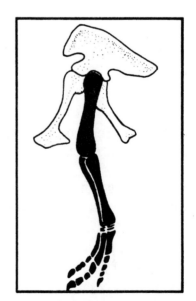

Saurians
lizard-hipped

2) In the *Saurian* order, the animals' hindquarters are like those of lizards. This group includes all the meat eaters, plus giant plant eaters, such as the *Diplodocus*.

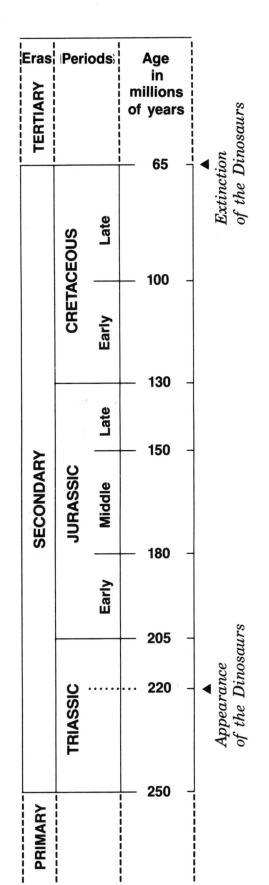

Eras	Periods		Age in millions of years

<table>
<tr><td rowspan="9">SECONDARY</td><td colspan="2"></td><td></td></tr>
</table>

Eras / **Periods** / **Age in millions of years**

TERTIARY

— 65 — ◄ *Extinction of the Dinosaurs*

CRETACEOUS — Late

— 100 —

CRETACEOUS — Early

— 130 —

JURASSIC — Late

— 150 —

JURASSIC — Middle

— 180 —

JURASSIC — Early

— 205 —

TRIASSIC .... — 220 — ◄ *Appearance of the Dinosaurs*

— 250 —

PRIMARY

SECONDARY (era)

Dinosaurs inhabited the earth long before humans arrived. The first species of dinosaur appeared 220 million years ago! (And their ancestors went back to 400 or 500 million years ago—more about them later!)

Then, for 150 million years, there were more dinosaurs on earth than any other land animals. This period of time is known as "The Age of the Dinosaurs," or the Secondary Era, or the Mesozoic Era. Scientists divide it into three parts, as you can see from the table at the left: *Triassic, Jurassic, Cretaceous.*

Then the dinosaurs disappeared suddenly about 65 million years ago. So did the flying reptiles and marine reptiles. No one knows why for sure.

Some say the mysterious disappearance seems to be linked to a drop in temperature that could have been caused by a huge meteorite or comet crashing to earth. If this is what happened, immense dust clouds might have enveloped the planet for a long time, shutting out the rays of the sun. The cold might have killed many species of animals, including all the dinosaurs. Just a few reptile species survived, such as crocodiles, turtles, snakes and small lizards.

Prehistoric man did not appear until 60 million years after the last dinosaurs died. The silhouettes of adult humans shown in this book are there only to indicate the size of the animals.

So you can see why only bones and fossil imprints in rock or sand give us a clue about what dinosaurs and other extinct reptiles looked like. And it wasn't until the 1800s that *fossils* were discovered!

The study of extinct animals is called *paleontology* (pronounced pale-ee-un-TAH-luh-gee). It is one of the branches of geology, the study of the Earth, past, present and future, its materials, its workings, and its fossils.

1

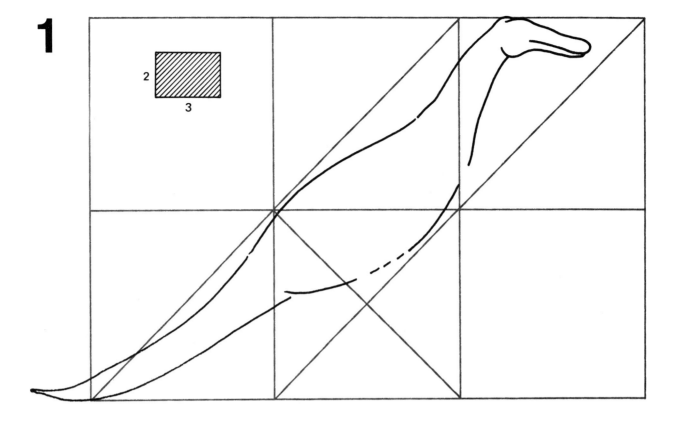

2

3

2

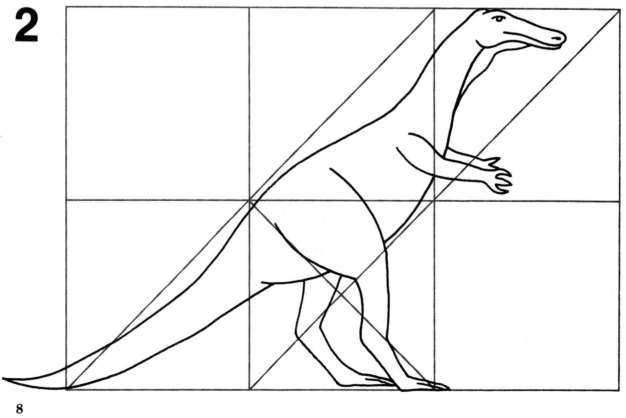

ANATOSAURUS
"Duck Lizard"

Its name comes from its skull and duck-shaped jaw.

This creature is a vegetarian and it is huge. It sometimes reaches a length of 39 feet (13 m).

Many fossils have been found of this species—usually in the form of skeletons—and sometimes even in the form of "mummies," their wrinkled skin turned to stone.

One of the last dinosaurs on our planet, it lived in North America, Europe and Asia, before it disappeared 65 million years ago.

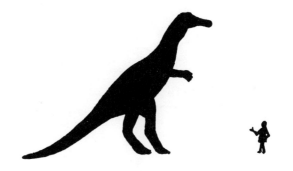

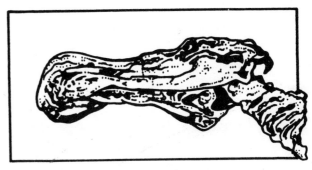

Mummified skull of an Anatosaurus

3

1

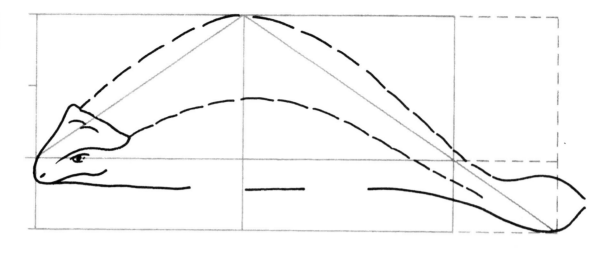

2

3

ANKYLOSAURUS
"Curved Lizard"

This reptile looks like a big armadillo. It was the largest armored dinosaur of its kind, sometimes measuring close to 20 feet (6 m) long.

Its body was entirely protected by bony plates that were connected to each other. With this solid shell, it could fight off the attacks of dangerous meat eaters such as the Tyrannosaurs. Basically a peaceful animal, it had even more defenses: a club-shaped tail and an armor-plated head!

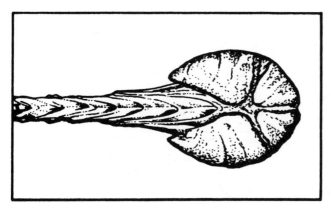

Fossil tail of an Ankylosaurus

Fossils of this animal have been found in the United States and Canada. They date from 65 to 100 million years ago.

Other armored dinosaurs from the Cretaceous Era

Polacanthus   Pinacosaurus   Euoplocephalus

1 yard (1 m)

1

2

BRACHIOSAURUS
"Arm Lizard"

Its name comes from its forelegs, which are much longer than its hind legs, so they look like arms.

This gigantic plant eater could reach a length of 75 feet (25 m) and a height of 36 feet (12 m). Some of them may have weighed as much as 88 tons (80 m tons)—the weight of 18 elephants!

Brachiosaurus disappeared from the planet 140 million years ago (during the Jurassic period). Its remains have been found in Africa (Tanzania) and in North America (Colorado).

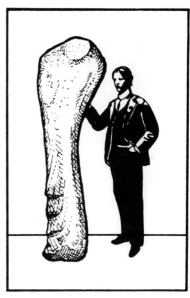

"Arm" (humerus) *of the* Brachiosaurus

3

1

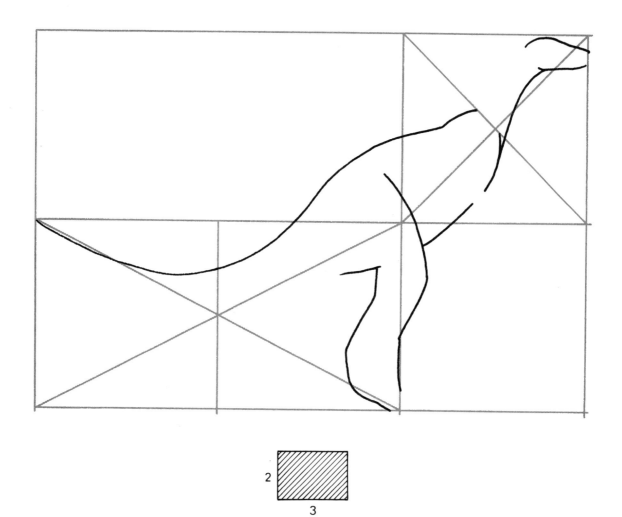

2 ▨ 3

2

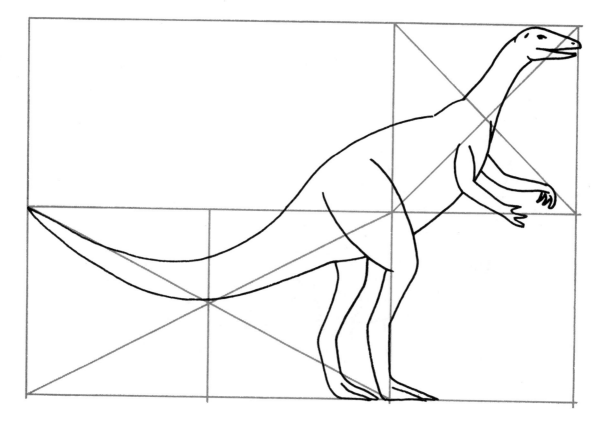

COMPSOGNATHUS
"Elegant Jaw"

This dinosaur was one of the smallest that ever lived. The adult measured less than three feet (1 m) long.

Its small (and pretty!) jaw proves that it was a meat eater, and the make-up of its stomach, as revealed by some fossils, is that of a lizard.

Detailed reconstruction of the head of the Compsognathus

Compsognathus was a two-footed dinosaur. It moved around by running on its hind legs.

Its traces have been found in France and Germany, in areas that date back 135 million years.

3

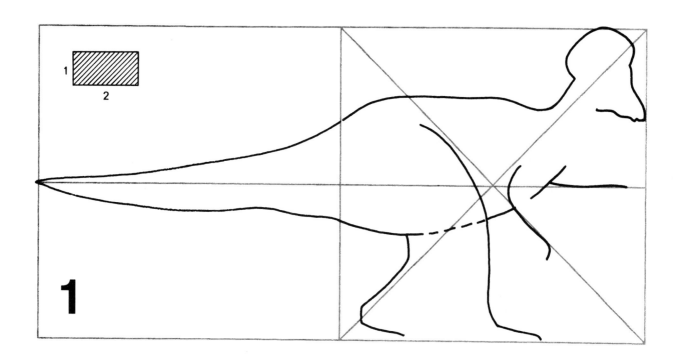

1

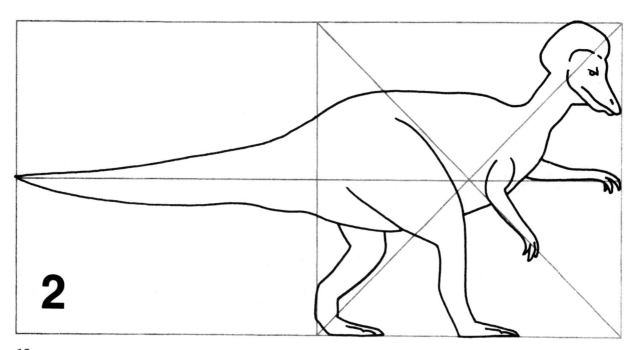

2

CORYTHOSAURUS
"Helmet Lizard"

This cousin of the *Anatosaurus* also had a duck jaw, but you can recognize it easily by the bony, grooved crest at the top of its skull.

Corythosaurus (pronounced cory-tho-SORE-us) was a peaceful plant eater. Its crest, which stretched all the way down to its nostrils, gave it an excellent sense of smell, so that it could detect its enemies from far away.

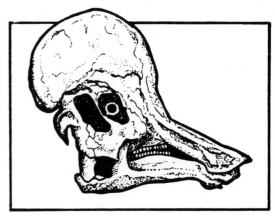

Fossil skull of a Corythosaurus

The fossils of *Corythosaurus* show that it was about 30 feet (10 m) long. They have been found in western Canada, where it lived more than 65 million years ago.

3

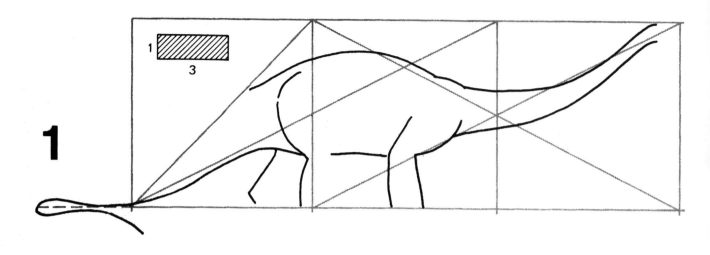

1

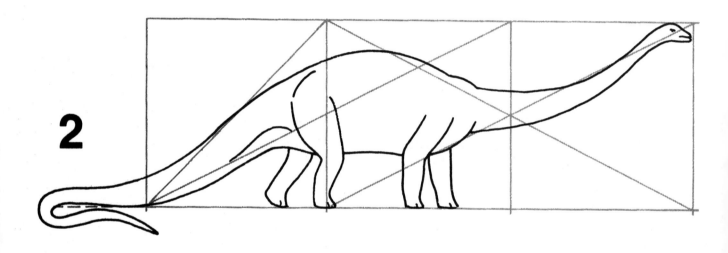

2

3

18

DIPLODOCUS
"Double Beam"

One of the most famous dinosaurs, *Diplodocus* gets its name from its strange spinal column, formed of double bones.

Diplodocus could reach a length of 100 feet (30 m), but more than half of that consisted of its tail. This big and heavy North American plant eater—27 tons (25 m tons)—spent most of its time in lake water, like the hippopotamus.

Scientists believe that *Diplodocus*, like the other great dinosaurs, had a lifespan of several centuries. It disappeared 141 million years ago.

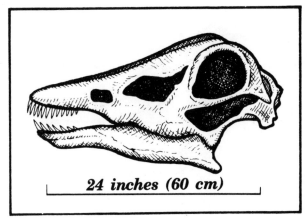

24 inches (60 cm)

Skull of a Diplodocus

The popularity of *Diplodocus* is due to the American millionaire Andrew Carnegie (1835–1919), who financed research on it. He even had casts made of this animal, which he offered to the world's great museums.

The complete scientific name of this famous dinosaur is *Diplodocus carnegiei.*

1

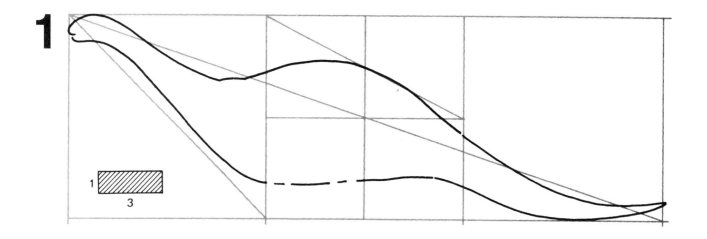

1 ▨
3

2

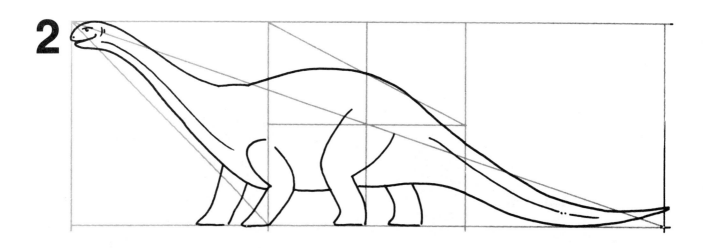

3

HYPSELOSAURUS
"Tall Lizard"

This large four-legged plant eater was about 40 feet (12 m) long. It was a "cousin" of *Diplodocus*, but *Diplodocus* disappeared 75 million years earlier. This means that more time passed between the lifetimes of these two dinosaurs than all the time between the disappearance of the *Hypselosaurus* and the coming of Man—that's more than 600,000 centuries!

Among other remains, *Hypselosaurus* has left its eggs. Their actual size was only 10 or 12 inches (25–30 cm), but they are the largest reptile eggs ever found. The discovery of other, smaller dinosaur eggs proves that the size of the egg has no relation to the size of the animal. Giant reptiles twice as large as the *Hypselosaurus* did not have eggs that were twice as big.

The eggs of the *Hypselosaurus* had a double limestone shell. The inner shell was a little less than one eighth of an inch thick (2 mm), and the outer shell was just a little bit thicker (3 mm).

The eggs and bones of the *Hypselosaurus* have been found in France, where it seems to have been the largest dinosaur. It was one of the last dinosaurs to disappear—65 million years ago.

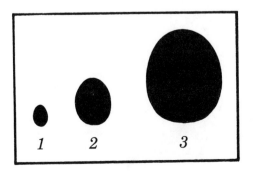

Comparison of egg sizes

1) Chicken

2) Ostrich

3) Hypselosaurus

1

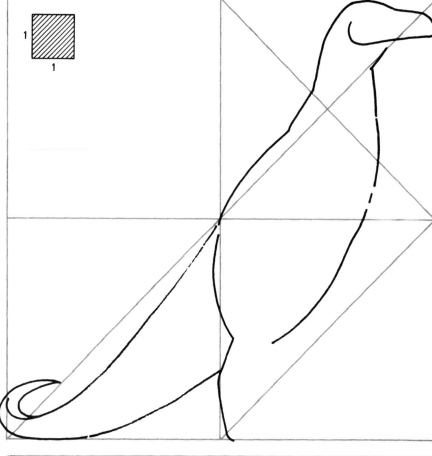

2

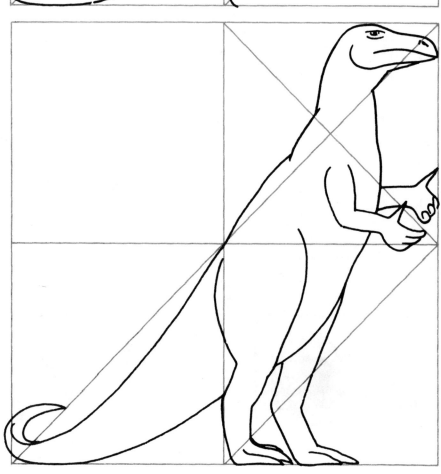

IGUANODON
"Iguana Tooth"

Iguanodons walked on two legs. They were plant eaters, as their teeth indicate. Their teeth look like those of today's iguana, a small reptile that lives in the tropics of the Americas and is about 5 feet (1.5 m) long.

Several different types of *Iguanodons* have been found. Its numerous fossils have been discovered in Belgium, Great Britain and France. The tallest species reached a height of 16–20 feet (5–6 m), and they were about 33 feet (10 m) long. Other species were no larger than 13 feet (4 m) tall and 20 feet (6 m) long.

The *Iguanodons* lived between 135 million and 110 million years ago.

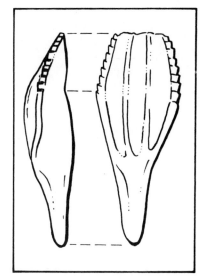

Iguanodon *tooth*

3

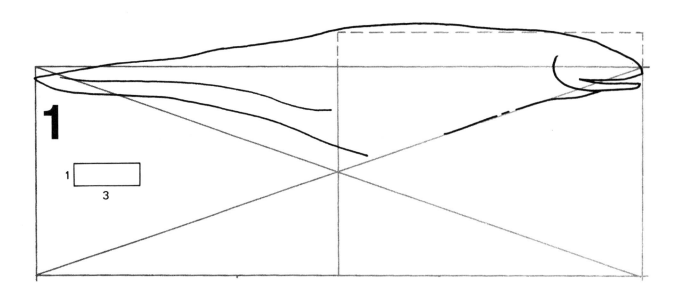

1

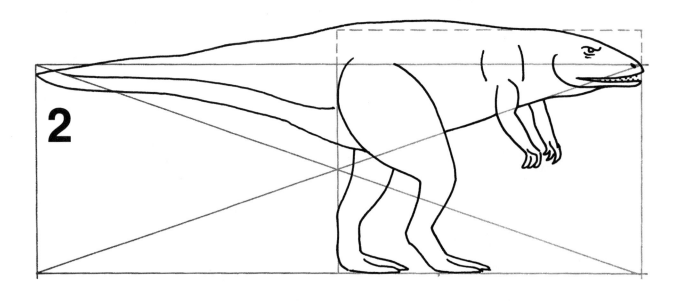

2

3

24

MEGALOSAURUS
"Great Lizard"

In 1824 the bones and the jaw of an unknown animal were discovered in England. The animal was named *Megalosaurus*, meaning in Greek, "Great Lizard."

Many fossils of *Megalosaurus* have been found since then. A terrifying meat eater, it survived by hunting down and eating other, more peaceful dinosaurs. This creature could reach about 30 feet (9 m) in length.

The teeth of the *Megalosaurus* are curved, like a saber, with cutting notches on the edges.

You can recognize this two-footed reptile by its short front "arms," with powerful claws that could move in and out to capture its prey.

Various species of *Megalosaurus* lived all over our planet during a very long period that began about 180 million years ago. The *Megalosaurus*, like the other dinosaurs, disappeared 65 million years ago.

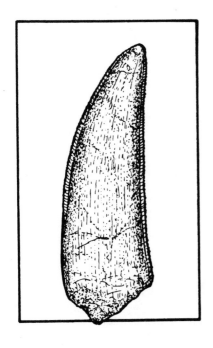

Tooth of a Megalosaurus—4½ inches (11 cm) long

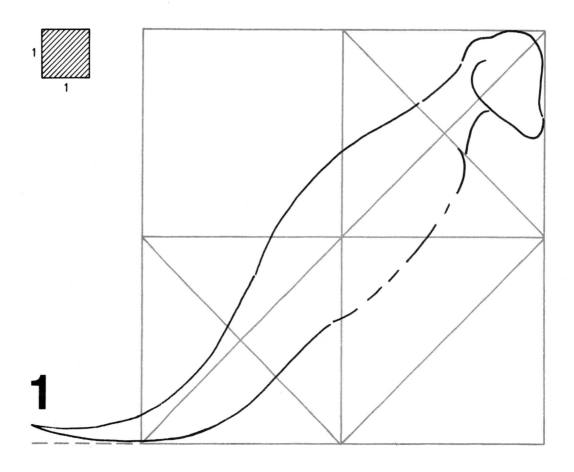

1

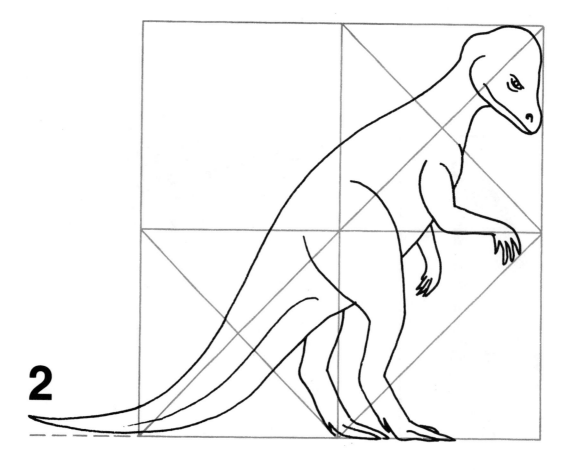

2

PACHYCEPHALOSAURUS
"Thick-Headed Lizard"

Here's an easy way to pronounce the name of this dinosaur:

pakka-seffa-lo-SORE-us.

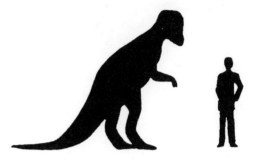

Looking at this animal, you can see why scientists named it "thick-headed." These plant eaters had headpieces that looked like a bony helmet, which shows that they fought each other with their heads, just the way some present-day animals (rams, for example) do. These dinosaurs reached a length of 15 feet (4.5 m), so it must have been quite a sight when they battled among themselves.

They lived in North America, a little before the extinction of the dinosaurs—65 million years ago.

Skull of a Pachycephalosaurus

3

1

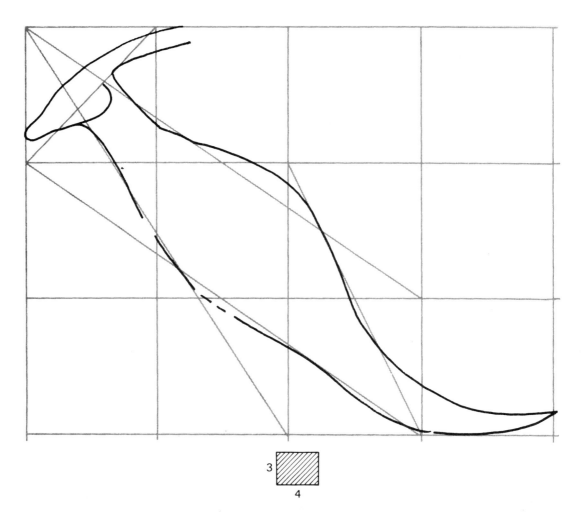

3 |////| 4

2

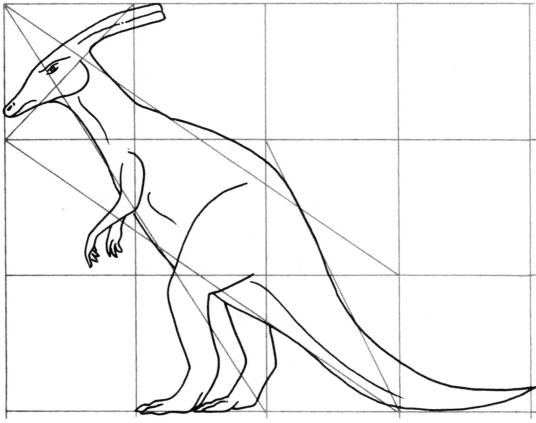

PARASAUROLOPHUS
"Beside the Crested Lizard"

The name of this dinosaur (pronounced para-sore-a-LO-fus) comes from the name of another dinosaur—*Saurolophus*—which also had a crest at the peak of its skull. The hollow "horn" opened into this animal's nose, so its sense of smell was probably excellent.

Head of a
Saurolophus
(crested lizard)

These duck-jaw dinosaurs belonged to the same family as the *Anatosaurus*, but they never got larger than 33 feet (10 m) long.

They lived in North America (Canada and the United States) a little more than 65 million years ago.

3

1

3 □ 4

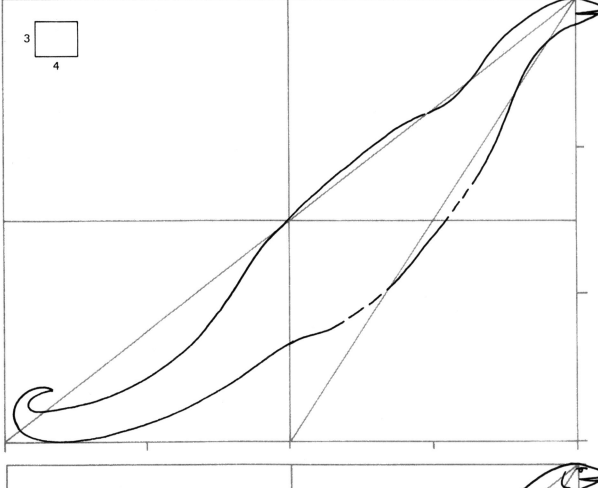

2

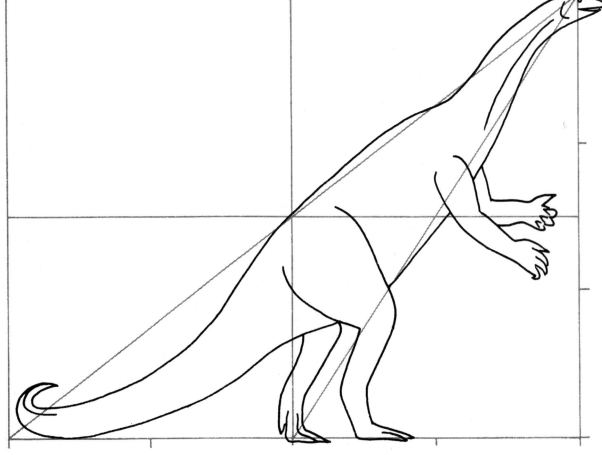

PLATEOSAURUS
"Large Lizard"

This is one of the most ancient dinosaurs known. It measured almost 30 feet (9 m) long when it stood on all four legs, and more than 13 feet (4 m) tall when it stood on its hind legs.

Plateosaurus travelled in herds. We know this because its fossils were found in groups in what looked like dinosaur cemeteries.

Their remains have been found in Germany, France and Switzerland, where they lived 200 million years ago.

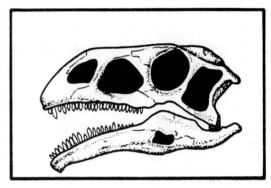

Skull of a Plateosaurus

3

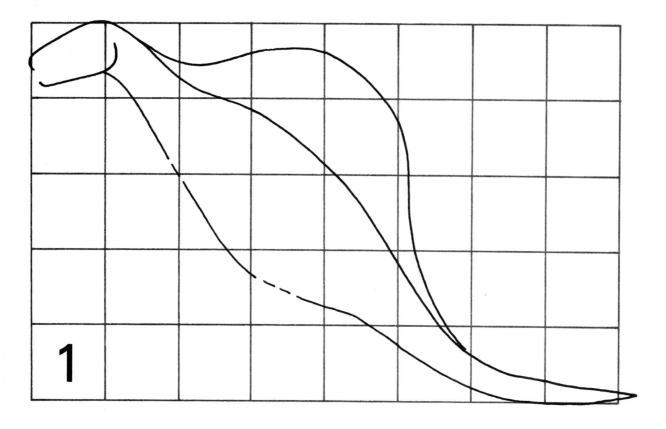

1

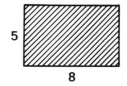

5

8

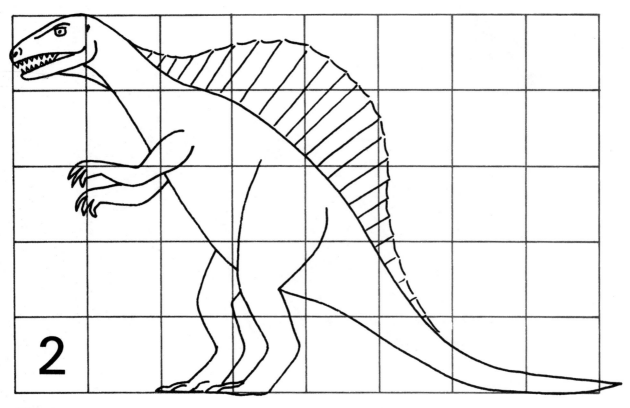

2

SPINOSAURUS
"Spiny Lizard"

This dinosaur could measure up to 46 feet (14 m) long, and it had very spiny bones coming from its spine, with a sail-like skin stretched over them. It gets its name from these spines.

Spinosaurus was an impressive meat eater, sometimes weighing more than 7 tons (6 m tons).

Its remains were found in Egypt. They date from a little more than 65 million years ago.

Like all the other meat-eating dinosaurs, *Spinosaurus* was a reptile with lizard hips.

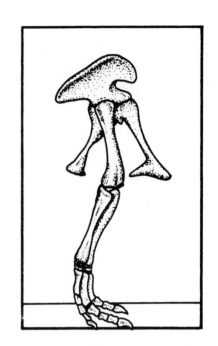

3

1

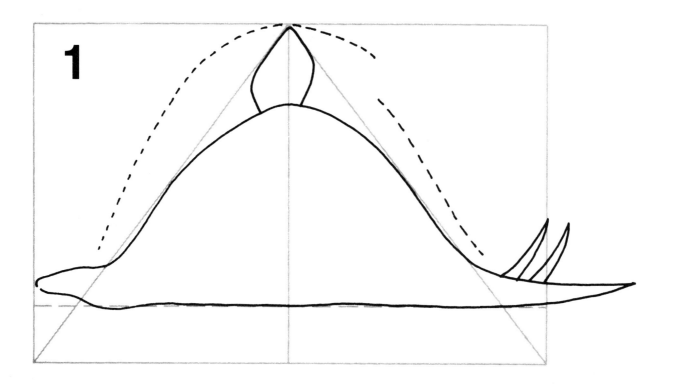

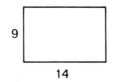

9

14

2

34

STEGOSAURUS
"Roof Lizard"

This dinosaur had a series of bony plates along the top of its back and sharp, pointed barbs on its tail.

The largest member of the stegosaur family could reach 30 feet (9 m) in length. Its brain was tiny—the size of a billiard ball—indicating that the *Stegosaurus* was very slow and placid, just capable of grazing on the vegetation that it found within reach.

The *Stegosaurus* lived in North America 140 million years ago. Some animals from the same family, measuring between 12 and 16 feet (3.5 and 5 m) long, have been found in Europe, mostly in France and Great Britain.

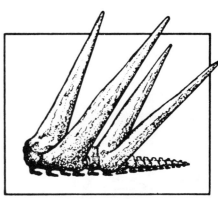

Fossilized tail of a Stegosaurus

3

1

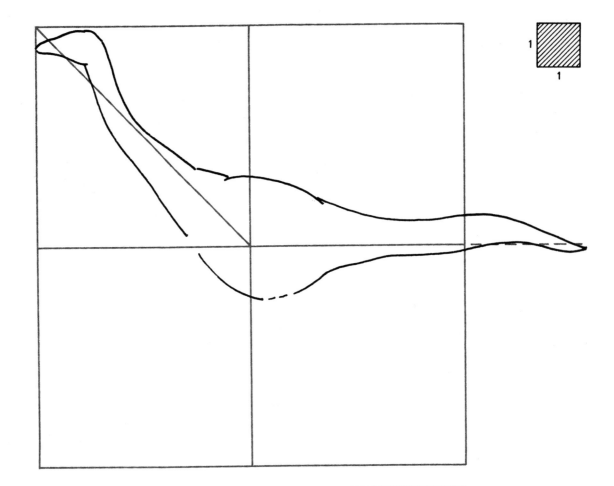

2

36

STRUTHIOMIMUS
"Ostrich Mimic"

Here's a dinosaur whose silhouette—and especially its tail—may remind you of an ostrich. *Struthiomimus*, 12 feet (3.5 m) in length, had a long neck, and a head that had a horned toothless beak. It's believed that this animal fed itself mostly on the eggs of insects and other reptiles.

Struthiomimus lived in North America about 80 million years ago.

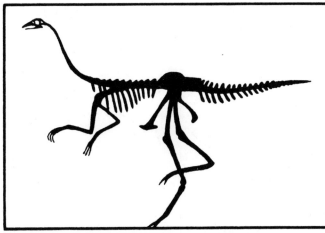

Skeleton of Struthiomimus

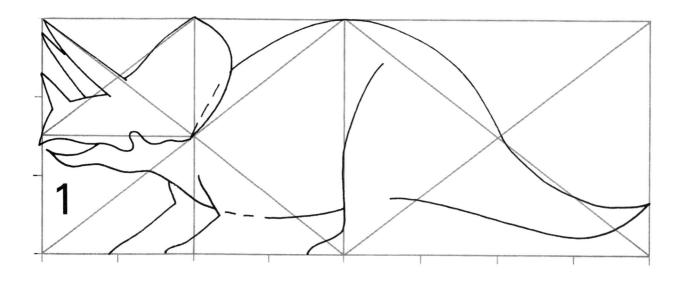

1

2

3	
8	

3

TRICERATOPS
"Three-Horned Face"

This large plant eater, whose head had three horns, also had a large bony "ruff" that covered its neck. Because of this, its skull measured 8 feet (2.5 m) by itself. The ruff protected it from its enemies, such as the tyrannosaur.

To visualize a living triceratops, picture a gigantic rhinoceros, measuring more than 33 feet (10 m) in length and weighing almost 10 tons (9 m tons). That's three times longer and six times heavier than the present-day rhinoceros.

Like other dinosaurs, this enormous beast was a reptile, and the female laid eggs.

Fossils of *Triceratops* have been found in North America, western Canada, and the western United States. These animals lived at the end of the "Age of the Dinosaurs," more than 65 million years ago.

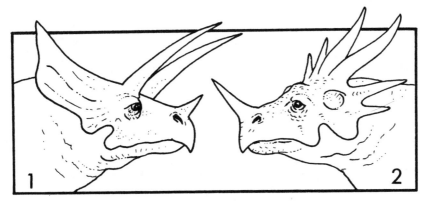

Similar to the* Triceratops *are:

1) Torosaurus *("Bull Lizard")*

2) Styracosaurus *("Spurred Lizard")*

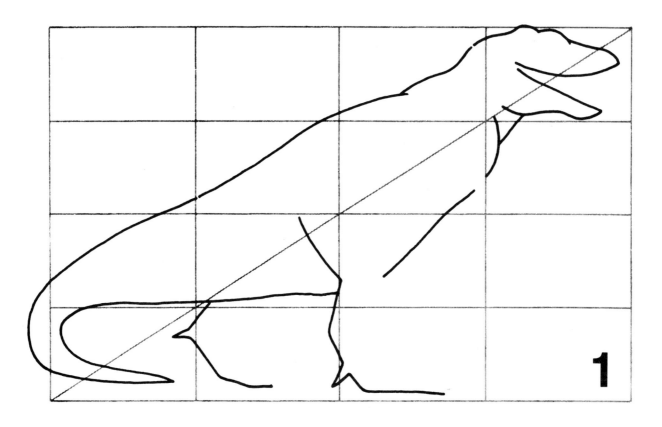

1

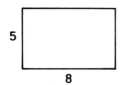

5

8

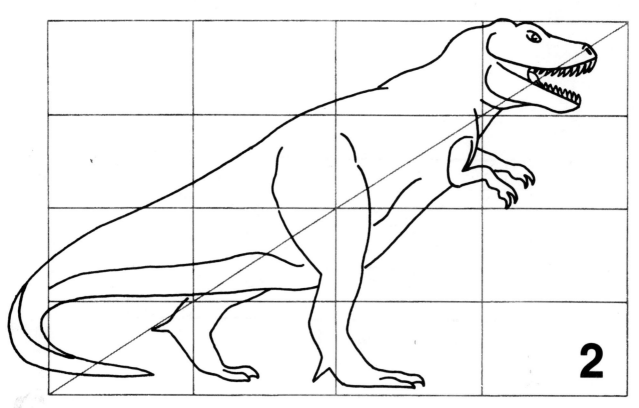

2

TYRANNOSAURUS
"Tyrant Lizard"

This was the largest meat eater known. 20 feet (6 m) tall and 50 feet (15 m) long, this terrible dinosaur was feared by every dinosaur alive.

Its powerful jaw was armed with thin, sharp and pointed teeth that were up to 8 inches (20 cm) long. Its forelegs—with its two long, clawed fingers—were very small compared to its hind legs. These hind legs gave it a long stride of 13 feet (4 m).

The bones of this meat eater have been found in North America (United States and Canada), and in central Asia (the former Soviet Union). *Tyrannosaurus* was one of the last dinosaurs to live on our planet before they all disappeared more than 65 million years ago.

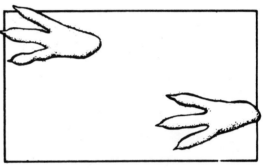

Fossilized footprints of the Tyrannosaurus

3

1

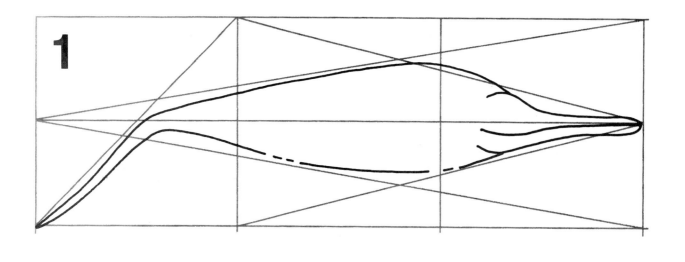

2

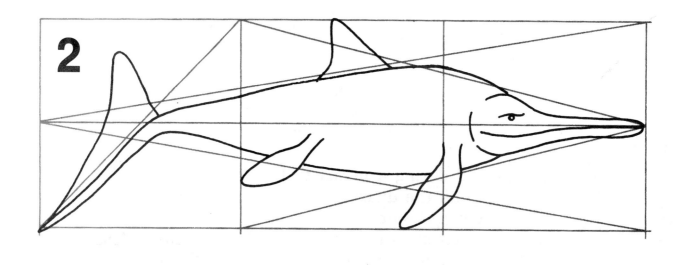

3

ICHTHYOSAURUS
"Fish Lizard"

Marine Reptile

Does this creature look familiar? No, it's not a dolphin—it's an *ichthyosaur* (pronounced IK-thee-a-sore). It was very well adapted to living in the sea.

Its teeth indicate that it was a meat eater. It ate other fish, shellfish, and even other *ichthyosaurs* (young or weak ones). These reptiles didn't lay eggs: their newborn, like the dolphin's, were born directly into the water. The dolphin, however, is a mammal that is suckled by its mother, and *ichthyosaurs* were reptiles that produced no milk and had to feed themselves with food products from the sea.

The *ichthyosaurs* lived during a period that began 220 million years ago and ended when all the dinosaurs disappeared 65 million years ago. The most ancient *ichthyosaurs* were the smallest—3 feet (1 m) long, while the more recent (rarer) reached 33 feet (10 m) in length. Beautiful fossils and "mummies" have been found in Europe and in North America.

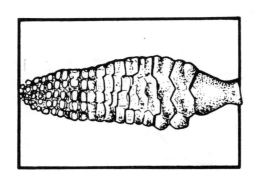

Skeleton of a front fin of an ichthyosaur

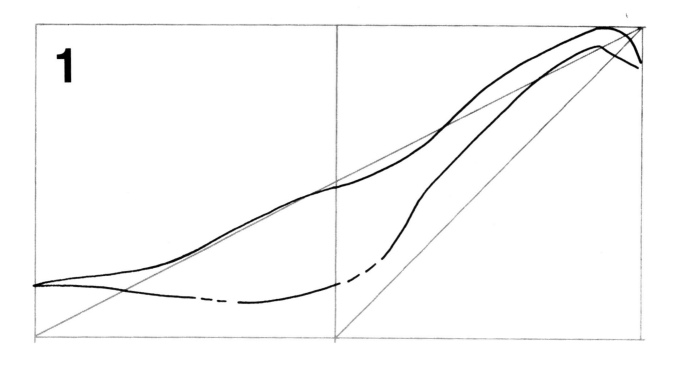

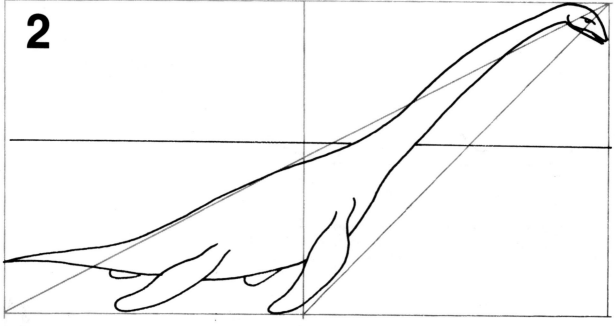

PLESIOSAURUS
"Close to a Lizard"

The *Plesiosaurus* was a neighbor of the *Ichthyosaurus*, with whom it lived, not far off the coasts. You can recognize it by its very long neck and short tail.

Like present-day seals, the *Plesiosaurus* swallowed pebbles* so it could digest its prey (fish and mollusks) more easily.

Populating the ocean shorelines for 130 million years, the *Plesiosaurus* disappeared 65 million years ago, at the same time as the dinosaurs, the pterosaurs and the ichthyosaurs. The size of this animal varied greatly, between 3 and 50 feet (1 and 15 m). Its traces have been found in America, and in Australia.

*These pebbles are called *gastroliths* (this name comes from two Greek words: *gastros* for belly, and *lithos* for stone).

Marine Reptile

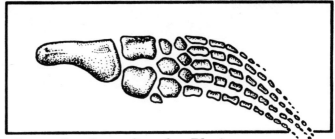

Bone of a front fin of a Plesiosaurus

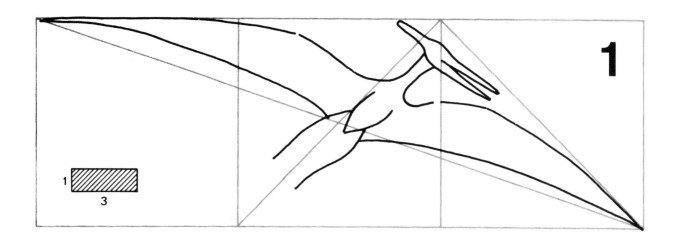

1

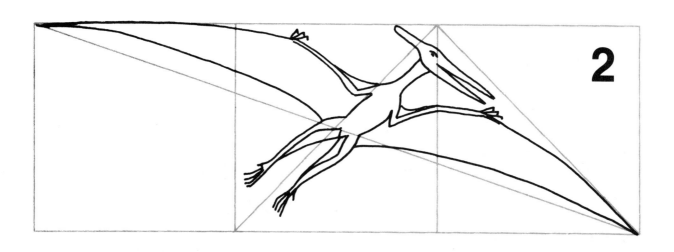

2

3

PTERANODON
"Winged Toothless"

The *Pteranodon* is a flying reptile from the *Pterosaurian* order, which includes species whose sizes range from a tiny shrew to an airplane with 40 feet (12 m) of wing-span! The word *pterosaurian* comes from a Greek word meaning "winged lizards."

These flying animals lived at the same time as the dinosaurs. They look a little like bats, but their wings were attached to a single long finger that grew out of their arms. Their other fingers formed little hands with claws that were outside of their wings.

We can tell that the *Pteranodon* was a fish eater from the fossilized fish that are sometimes found in its body. This reptile could sometimes reach 23 feet (7 m) in wing-span. Its fossils have been found in North America and in Russia, and they date from 100 million to 65 million years ago, when the dinosaurs disappeared.

Other *pterosaurs* lived before the dinosaurs or at the same time in other regions of the globe—in Germany, France, and Italy and in Africa.

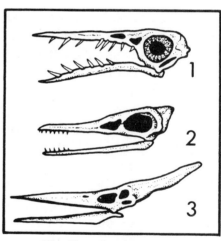

Skulls of pterosaurs

1) Ramphorhynchus

2) Pterodactylus

3) Pteranodon

And Before the Dinosaurs—
The Primitive Vertebrates

The Earth was formed around 4½ billion years ago. The first traces of life showed up one billion years later in the ocean. They had just a single cell and you could only see them with a microscope. These single-cell animals were the origin of all animal and vegetable species on our planet.

Then, only (!) 650 million years ago, much more complex animals appeared. They all had soft bodies: they were worms, sponges, and jellyfish. They still lived in the ocean because the atmosphere on land didn't contain enough oxygen for them to be able to breathe.

In the Cambrian Epoch

The first animals with shells appeared 540 million years ago and survived for about 40 million years. They were kinds of fish—so primitive that they didn't have jaws! For this reason, they're called *Agnatha*, which means "jawless" in Greek. They were the ancestors of all the fish, amphibians, reptiles, birds, and all mammals, including humans. Aside from birds, which separated from the reptile branch after the first mammals appeared, all these classes make up our personal family tree. So, if someone says that you're descended from a monkey, you tell them that, actually, you also have reptile, amphibian, fish and agnatha ancestors.

In the Devonian Epoch

Four hundred million years ago, the air became breathable. Certain fish adapted little by little to a life outside the water. The shape of their bodies didn't change right away, but their fins became five-toed feet. The first walking vertebrates (animals with a backbone) were amphibians. That means they sometimes lived in the water, where they laid their eggs, and sometimes out of it, like frogs do today.

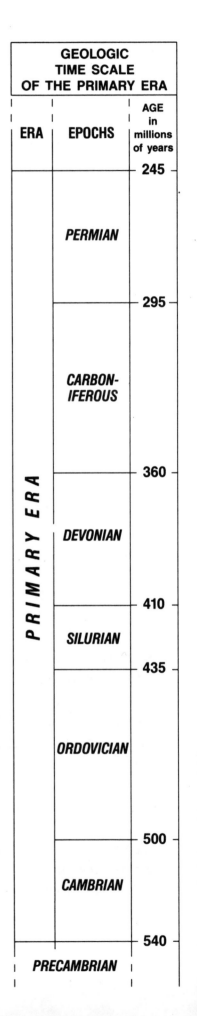

GEOLOGIC TIME SCALE OF THE PRIMARY ERA		
ERA	EPOCHS	AGE in millions of years
		— 245
	PERMIAN	
		— 295
	CARBON-IFEROUS	
		— 360
PRIMARY ERA	DEVONIAN	
		— 410
	SILURIAN	
		— 435
	ORDOVICIAN	
		— 500
	CAMBRIAN	
		— 540
	PRECAMBRIAN	

Three hundred million years ago, some of these animals left the water completely. They became reptiles. Reptiles lay their eggs on dry land. These eggs, like those of today's chickens and crocodiles, were made up of a white part and a yellow part, so that the embryo could feed and grow all by itself inside the eggshell. Unlike amphibians, the reptiles' skin doesn't dry out in the open air.

By the end of the Primary Era, the fish and the reptiles had evolved a great deal. The fish already looked the way fish look today. Some reptiles already had some of the characteristics of mammals. Others became dinosaurs and birds!

The amphibians didn't have the same success: their descendants are frogs, toads, newts, and salamanders.

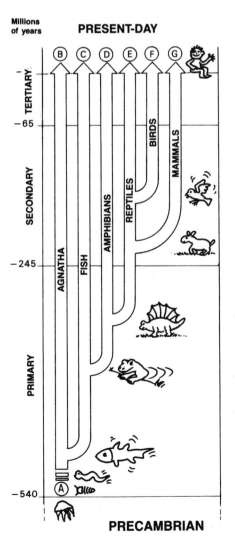

Fish

Amphibian

This very simplified chart shows how vertebrates evolved through time. Looking from A to each other letter (B to G), you can follow the progress of each kind of vertebrate.

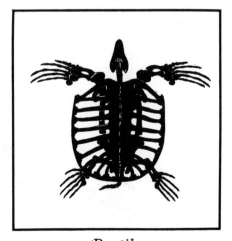

Reptiles

1

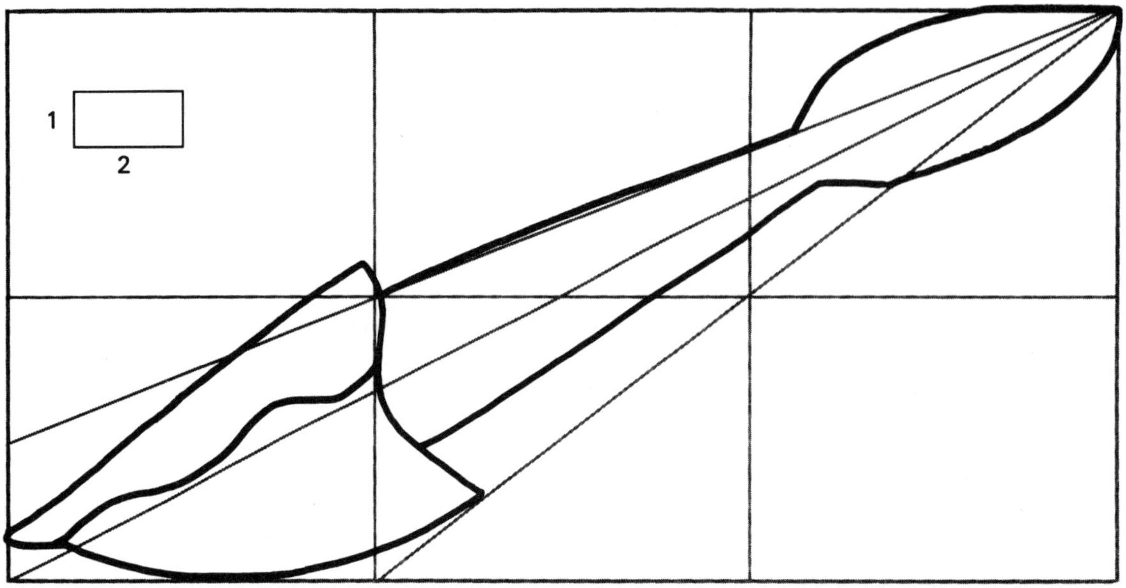

1 ▭
2

2

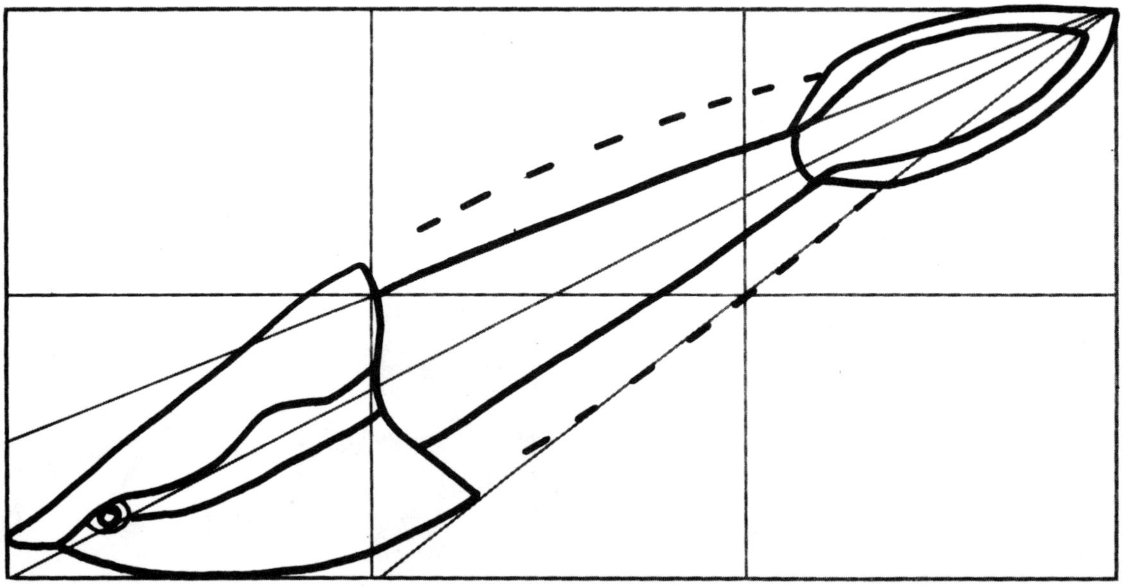

3

50

PORASPIS
"Orifice" and "Shield"

Poraspis belongs to the *Agnatha*, a class of animals whose name in Greek (*a* and *gnathos*) means "jawless". The *Agnatha* breathe mud and filter it in order to get their food from it.

Agnatha

Its mouth was a simple opening that sucked food in (orifice). Its body was protected by bony hinged plates (a shield).

Its armor protected it from its enemies, such as sea scorpions, which resembled giant lobsters (they sometimes reached 10 feet (3 m) long) or meat-eating mollusks, ancestors of the octopus or the nautilus.

Poraspis lived at the beginning of the Devonian era, about 400 million years ago, long before the first dinosaur.

Other fossils of Agnatha *have been found. Some look like these.*

1

3
4

2

3

DINICHTHYS
"Terrible Fish"

Dinichthys (pronounced din-IK-this) was a blood-thirsty fish with terrifying teeth. It came from the Placoderm family that took its name from the Greek words *plakos*, meaning "plate" and *derma*, meaning "skin." The front part of its body was protected by bony plates. This fish is also called the "armored fish."

Fish

It appeared 410 million years ago, just before the beginning of the Devonian epoch, and disappeared a little before the end of it, 360 million years ago. The main competitor of *Dinichthys* was the shark, which was a better swimmer and therefore a better hunter. As you know, the shark has survived to this day!

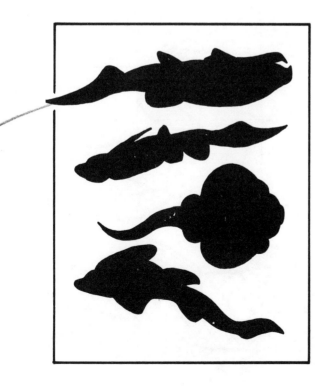

Silhouettes of other Placoderms

EUSTHENOPTERON
"Narrow Fins"

Fish

Can fish live out of water? This one did. It was one of the first vertebrates ever to leave the water.

In the Devonian epoch, 360 million years ago, there were droughts, and lakes and lagoons would often dry up. Of course, almost all the fish in them would die, except those that adapted to the situation—like *Eusthenoptron*. In addition to gills, it had lungs so it could breathe in the open air.

Since it didn't have feet, it was equipped with fleshy muscled fins. It used them for crawling. It would wallow in mud while waiting for the return of rain.

There are still some freshwater fish today that can breathe both in and out of water. They're called the *Dipnoi*, a word meaning "with two respirations." They live in the tropics.

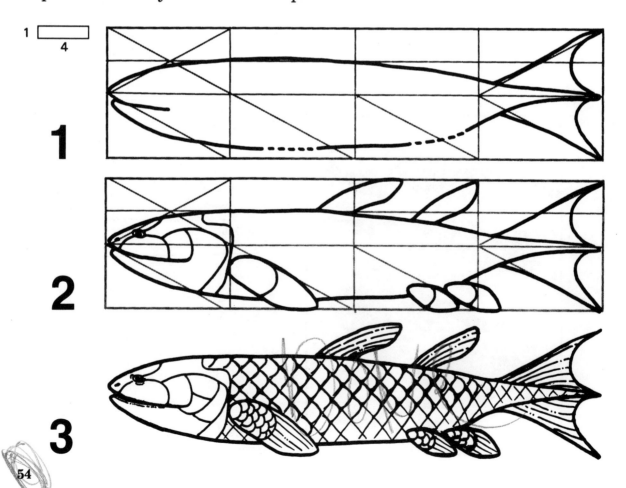

ICHTHYOSTEGA
"Fish Head"

Amphibian

Here's the first vertebrate to have real legs. Its walk was very clumsy. It swayed back and forth as it crept, aided by 5-toed feet.

Ichthyostega was not a fish, but the earliest known amphibian (animal that lives both in and out of the water, like frogs and salamanders). It comes after the *Agnatha* and the fish in the line of evolution.

Amphibians still depend on the water; they lay their eggs in it. Their tadpoles breathe with the help of gills, the way their fish ancestors did. Only later do they develop lungs and limbs.

The first amphibian fossil—360 million years old—was discovered in Greenland in 1928.

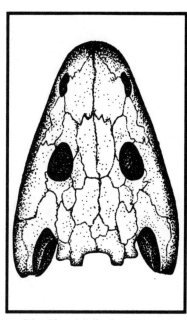

Skull of Ichthyostega

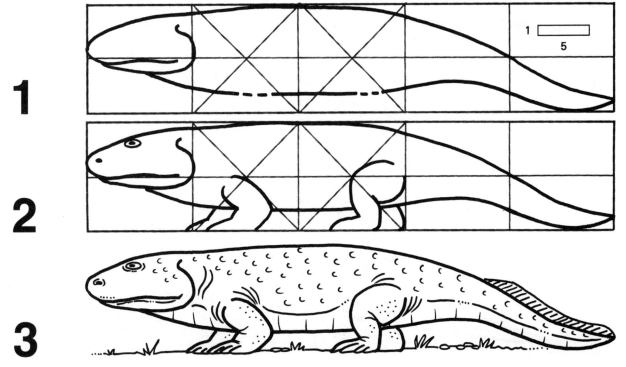

1

2

3

1

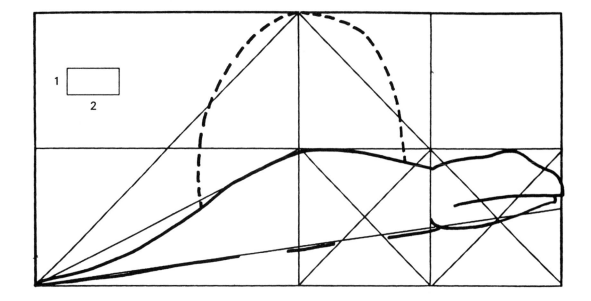

2

3

PLATYHYSTRIX
"Broad and Bristly"

Amphibian

This amphibian lived up to its name. Large and short-legged, its bony spine was very developed—it bristled from its body! The spiny spokes were linked by a sheet of skin.

Platyhystrix lived during the same period as *Edaphosaurus* (see page 70) and other reptiles who were equipped with a sail (page 72). Like other amphibians, *Platyhystrix* laid its eggs in water, where its "tadpoles" were born. This strange cousin of the frog measured 3 feet (1m) long as an adult.

Its fossil remains, 290 million years old, have been found in Texas.

Other forms of amphibians from the Primary Era

1

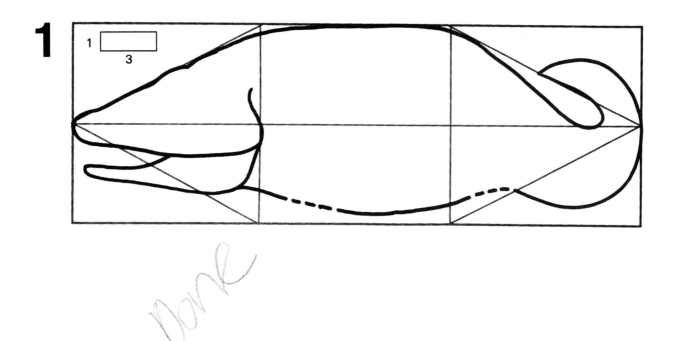

2

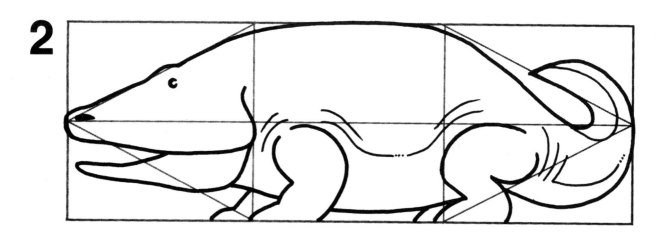

3

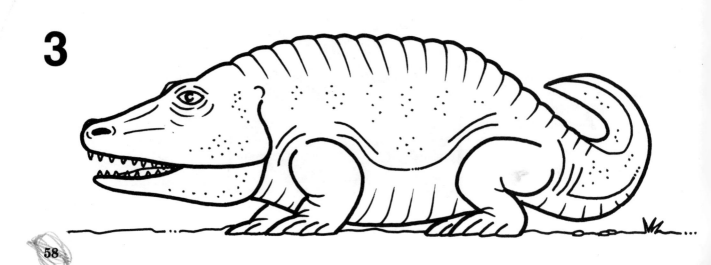

58

ERYOPS
"Stretch Face"

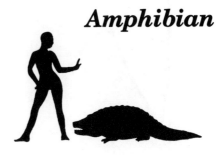

Amphibian

This massive amphibian, with short and powerful limbs, lived equally on dry land and in the water. We can tell it was a meat eater from its huge jaws and pointed teeth. It probably fed on both fish and land animals.

Its fossil remains, sometimes even complete skeletons, have been found in the southern United States in 280- to 300-million-year-old rocks. During that time, all of the planet's continents were on the verge of reassembling into one gigantic whole. When that happened several tens of millions of years later, the climate became drier, swamps became rarer—and *Eryops* disappeared! Similar animals, such as the smaller *Cacops* ("Evil Face")—16 inches (40cm) long, as opposed to the *Eryops'* 6½ feet (2m) long—adapted to the dry weather and outlasted *Eryops* by several million years. They became extinct about 240 million years ago.

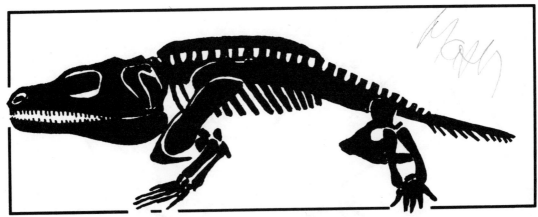

Skeleton of Cacops

1

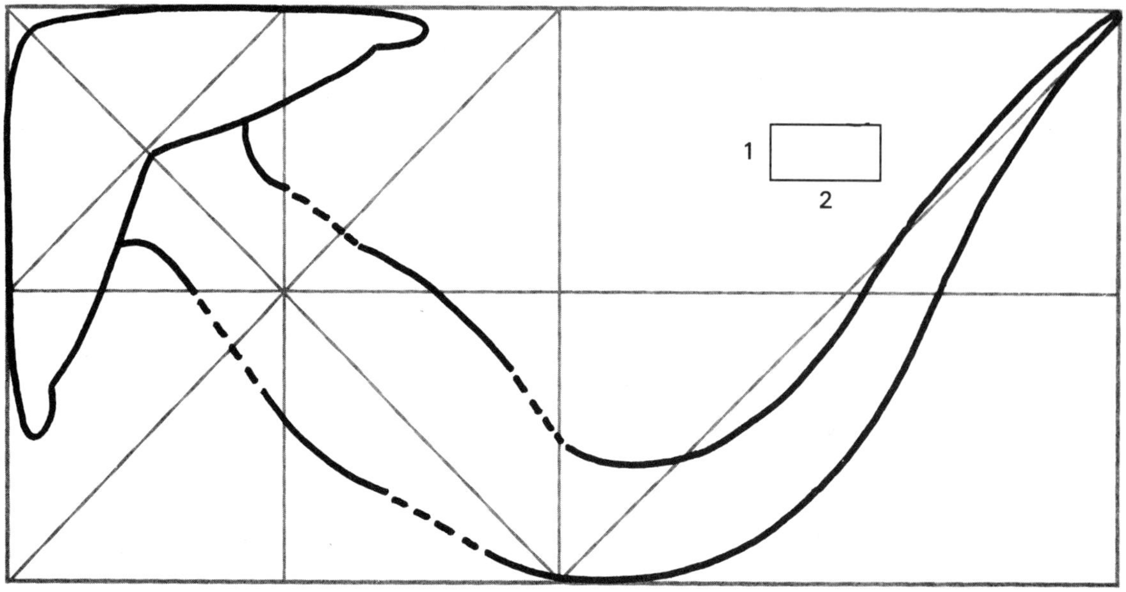

1
2

2

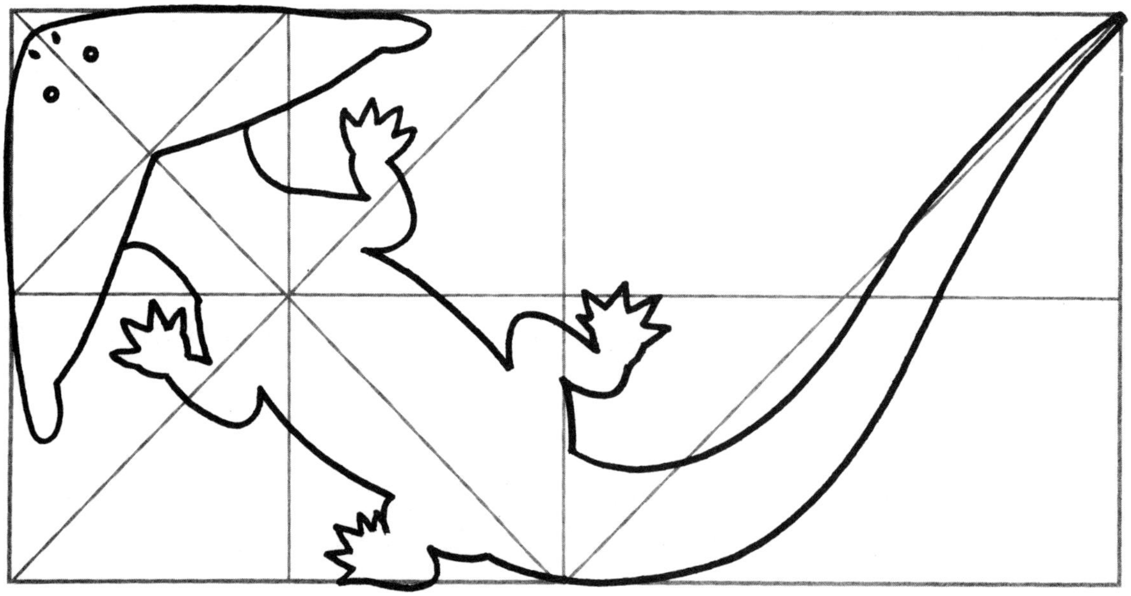

3

Done

60

DIPLOCAULUS
"Double Stem"

Amphibian

The skeleton of this odd amphibian was found in Texas.

It owes its name to its skull, which was very flat, with a bony spine on each side that was elongated towards the rear of its body. Viewed from above, its head was shaped like a triangle.

From the shape of *Diplocaulus's* body, especially its flat, fish-like tail, scientists deduced that it lived in ponds and lakes. Its fossils have been found in 300-million-year-old rocks. It disappeared about 275 million years ago, before the dinosaurs ever arrived.

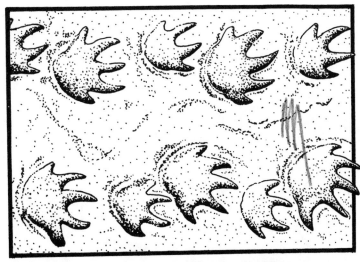

Tracks of a primitive amphibian

1

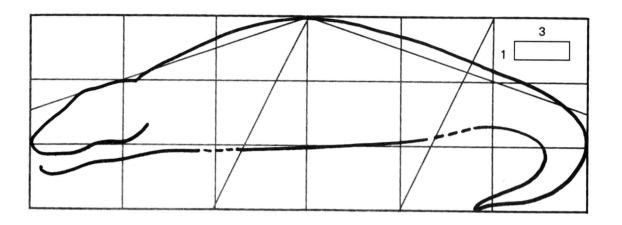

2

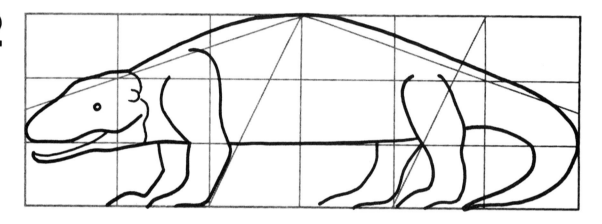

3

SEYMOURIA
"Seymour's Beast"

Amphibian

This little amphibian looks a lot
like a reptile. That's because its
way of life is a lot like the
reptile's. Less dependent on
water than other amphibians, its
limbs evolved to make it a better walker. *Seymouria* was the first
vertebrate to be equipped with longish legs, placed under its body.
These legs were useful during a time of wide-open spaces when all the
planet's continents formed one land mass. The climate had become so
dry that bodies of fresh water were rare. This explains *Seymouria's*
evolution 270 million years ago. It was named Seymour for a city in
Texas, near which its bones were found.

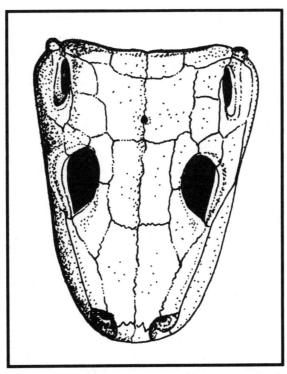

Skull of Seymouria

1

2

3

DIADECTES
"Who Bites Crosswise"

Amphibian

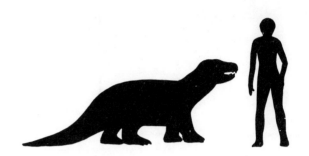

Some scientists consider this animal a link between amphibians and reptiles. Others don't. Certain bones from *Diadectes's* skeleton seem to prove that it lived on dry land, as most reptiles did. Others link it to the amphibians.

Its diet is still a mystery. Perhaps in the future, new fossils will be found that will tell us more about this puzzling creature.

The remains of *Diadectes* have been found in the United States in Texas, in rocks that go back 290 million years.

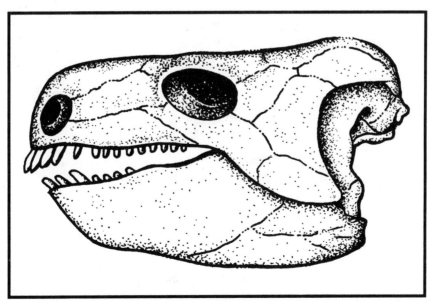

Skull of Diadectes

1

3 4

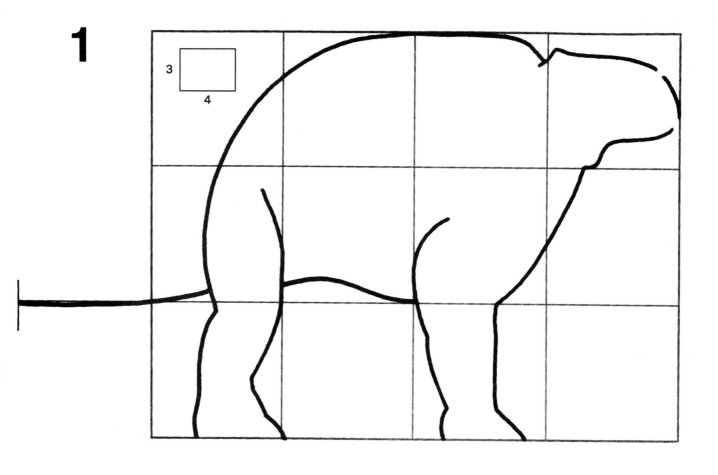

2

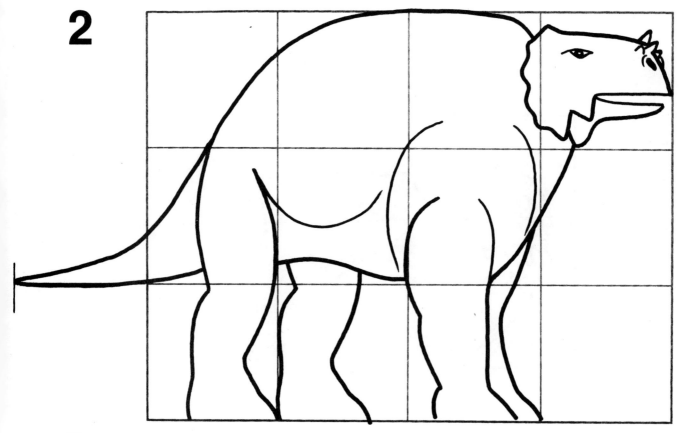

SCUTOSAURUS
"Shield-Lizard"

Reptile

This huge reptile was a plant eater, as you can tell from the shape of its teeth.

Its skull had bony outgrowths, and its back had plates that protected it like a shield.

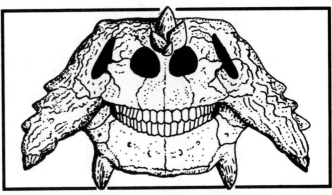

Skull of the Scutosaurus

The fossils of *Scutosaurus* have been found in Russia, but the remains of similar species have been found in South Africa. This confirms the theory that a single gigantic continent existed 245 million years ago at the end of the Primary Era, at about the same time that these animals disappeared.

3

1

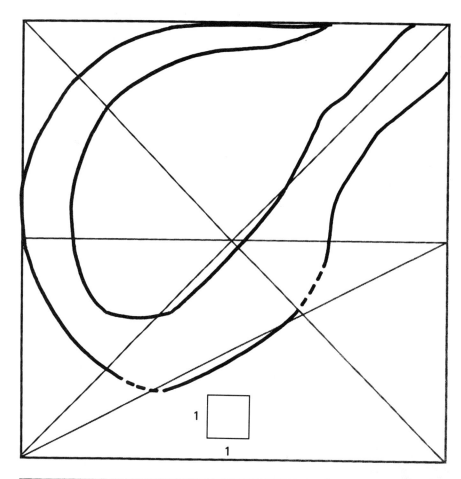

1 ▢
1

2

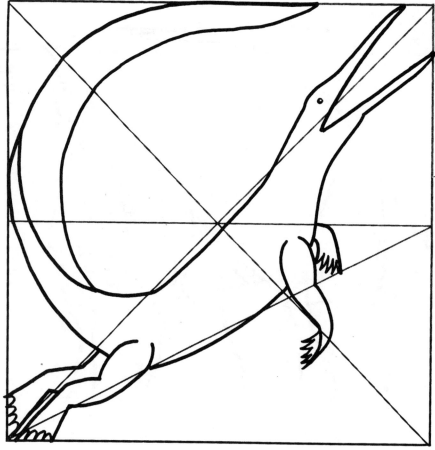

MESOSAURUS
"Intermediate Lizard"

Reptile

Mesosaurus is a reptile that breathed in air—and thus had lungs like other reptiles—but also had a long tail and webbed feet that helped it to propel itself easily in the water. It is the most ancient reptile known that went *back* to the water.

Its long, narrow head had many long teeth protruding from its jaws. They trapped the freshwater fish that *Mesosaurus* ate.

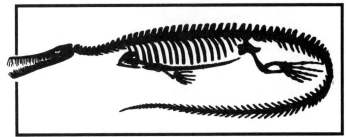

Skeleton of a Mesosaurus

Fossils of *Mesosaurus*, 270 million years old, have been found in South America and in Africa.

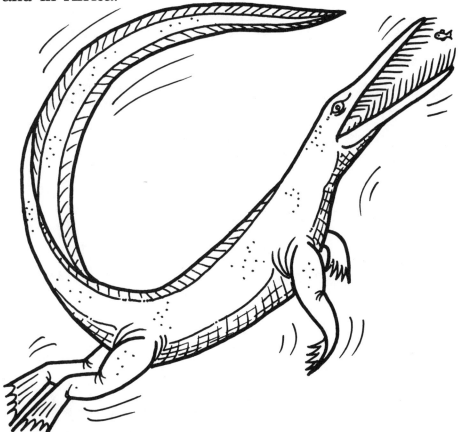

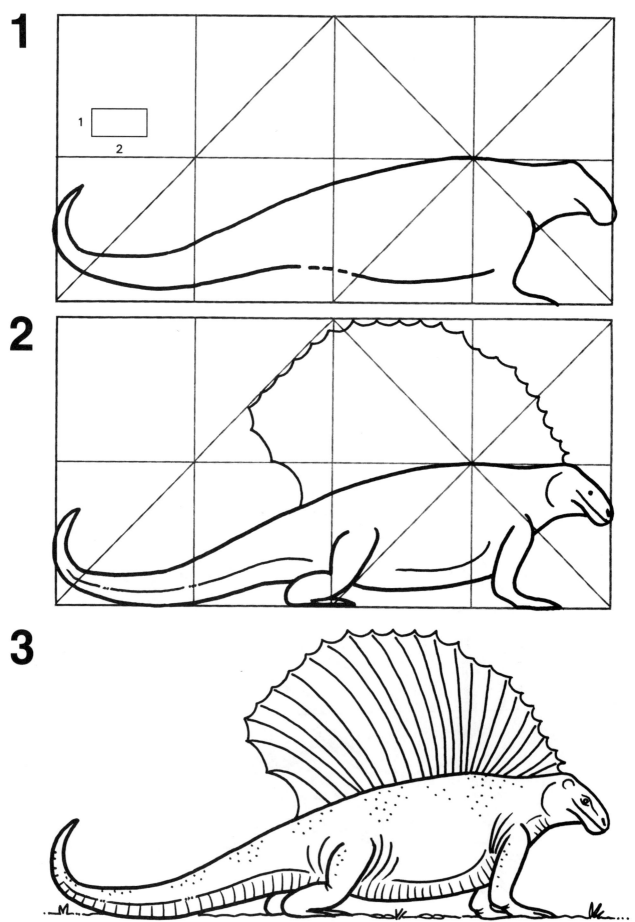

EDAPHOSAURUS
"Ground Lizard"

Reptile

This 11-foot (3.5m) long reptile had short limbs and a small skull, but its unique appearance is due, above all, to its "sail." This sail was skin that was attached to the very spiny bones on the animal's back. Scientists have suggested that the sail may have been a solar collector that provided energy to the animal's body, a sort of central heating system! Without this "climate control," these big cold-blooded reptiles would have been limited to living in warm places only.*

Heavy and lazy, *Edaphosaurus* ate the plants it found on the ground during its slow strolls. It was one of the very first plant eaters. It became extinct at the end of the Primary Era, 260 million years ago.

Skeleton of the Edaphosaurus

*For other animals with "sails," see pages 32, 56 and 72.

1

2

3

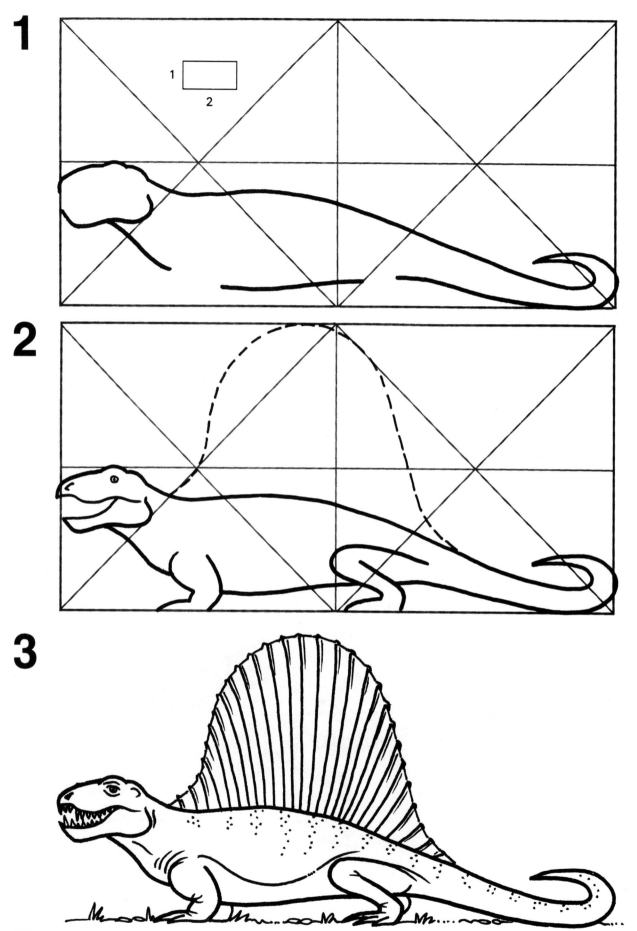

DIMETRODON
"Two Sizes of Teeth"

Reptile

Dimetrodon was the most common and the most famous reptile of the Primary Era. It is often considered—wrongly—a dinosaur. Several tens of millions of years passed between the disappearance of the *Dimetrodon* and the appearance of the first dinosaurs. Like its cousin the *Edaphosaurus* (pages 70 and 71), *Dimetrodon* had a "sail," very long bony spikes coming out of its back that had skin stretched over them.

Unlike *Edaphosaurus*, *Dimetrodon* was an aggressive meat eater, equipped with powerful jaws with cone-shaped teeth, slightly curved towards the rear. These teeth were of two different sizes, which is how the animal got its name.

Dimetrodon and *Edaphosaurus* appeared around 300 million years ago and disappeared more than 250 million years ago.

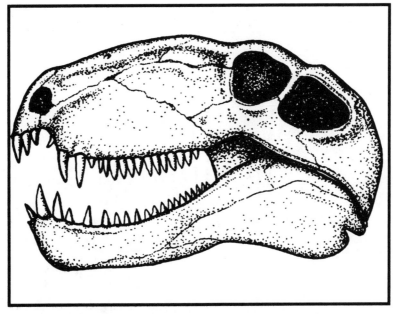

Skull of the Dimetrodon

73

1

2

3

74

BRADYSAURUS
"Slow Lizard"

Reptile

Everything about this animal was massive—except its teeth! A peaceful vegetarian, it came from a family of amphibious reptiles that lived like today's hippopotamus. Little by little, it adapted to the dry climate and eventually lived completely on land.

The thick, scaly skin of *Bradysaurus* protected it from its enemies—even from meat-eating reptiles. Its tail was short and its skull was particularly tough. *Bradysaurus* had no need to escape; it carried all its defensive armor with it. With so much protection, it could afford to be a *slow* lizard!

This creature from 270 million years ago was very primitive. Its vertebrae still resembled those of its fish ancestors. Yet, some of its bones suggest the mammals that we are!

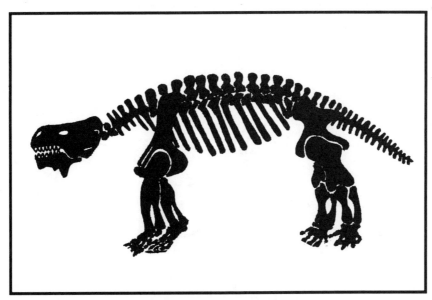

Skeleton of a Bradysaurus

1

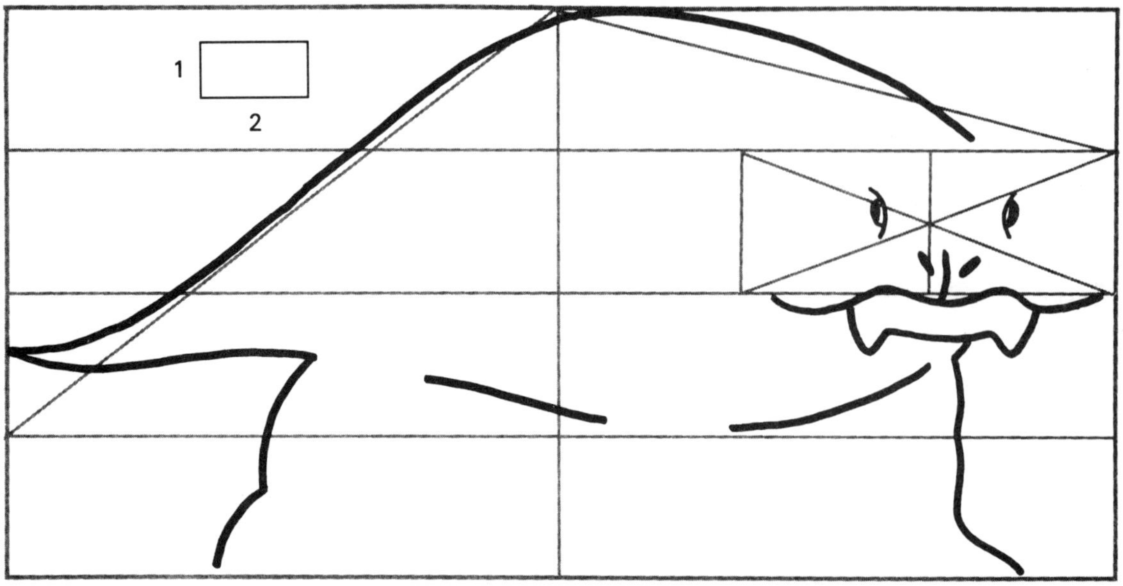

2

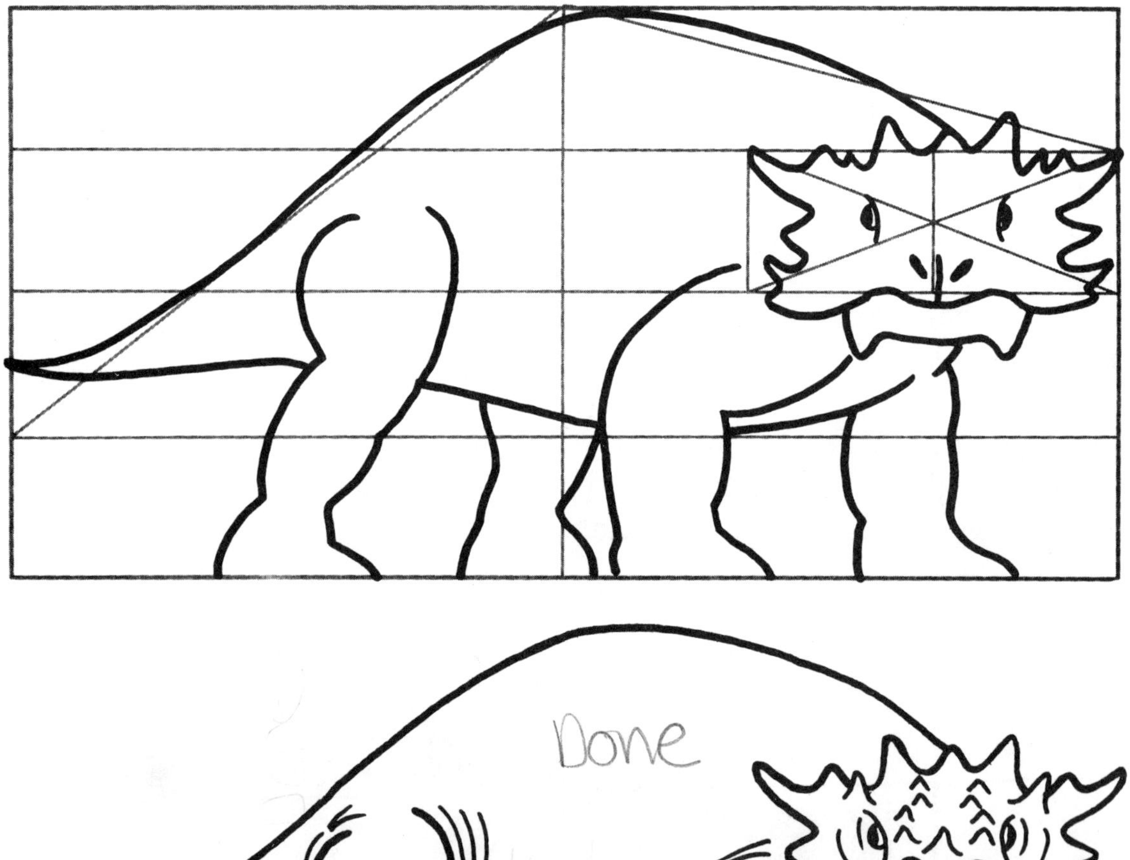

3

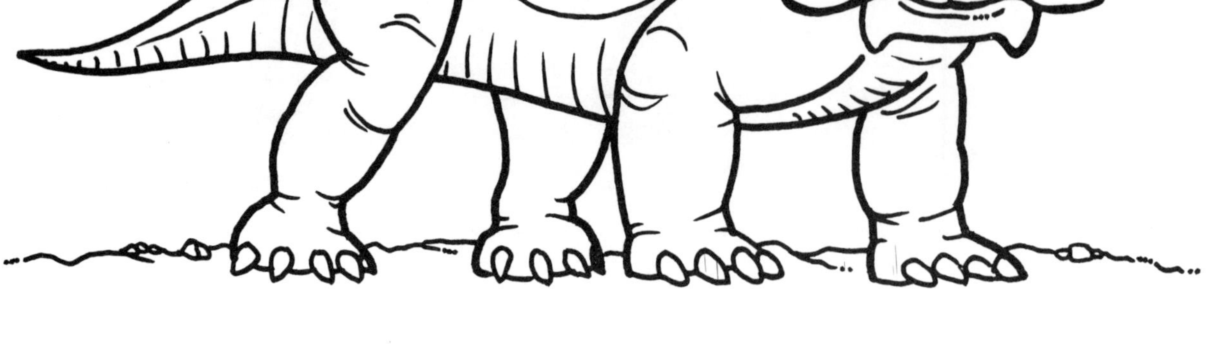

ELGINIA
"Reptile of Elginia"

Reptile

Great numbers of this very small animal appeared in South Africa at the end of the Primary Era and spread to northern Europe. No obstacle hampered its long journey, since all of the continents were joined together at the time.

Fossils of *Elginia* were found in Scotland, in the county of Elgin, which gave it its name.

It's thought that this strange-looking creature with its contorted skull led an amphibious existence, both on land and in the water, the way tortoises do today. This small plant eater measured 24 inches (60cm) long as an adult.

Elginia disappeared at the end of the Permian epoch, almost 250 million years ago.

Skull of Elginia

1

1
2

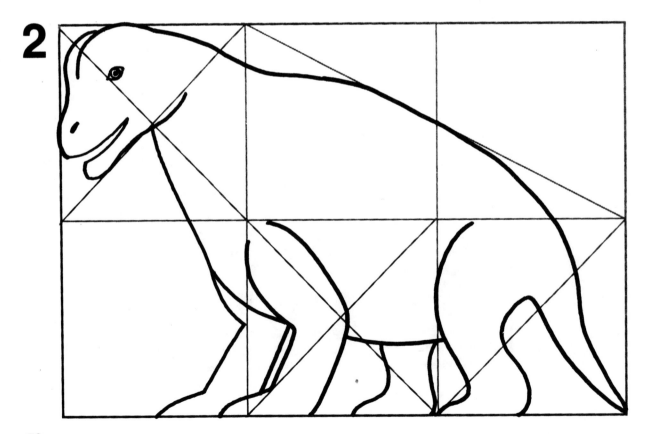

2

MOSCHOPS
"Calf Face"

Moschops was one of the largest reptiles of the Primary Era. It was usually about 10 feet (3m) long, but sometimes it could reach a length of 16 feet (5m). The size of its body was close to that of today's hippopotamus, but its front legs were much longer than its hind legs, giving it a very odd silhouette.

This huge reptile's teeth show that it grazed on the thick grass of South Africa. It was there that its 250-million-year-old fossil remains were found.

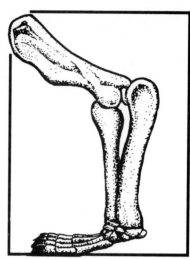

Front leg of Moschops

3

79

INDEX